Drama: Reading, Writing and Speaking Our Way Forward

Contents

Chapter 1	Looking at learning in classroom drama	1
	The development of the whole child	2
	Language and literacy development	3
	The development of the imagination	4
	The content of the drama	4
	The drama processes	4
	Reflection	5
Chapter 2	Drama in role play areas	6
	Child initiation and observation	6
	Teacher in role	7
	A real life context: a veterinary surgery	7
	A fictional setting: *We're Going on a Bear Hunt*	8
	A generic theme: a time machine	10
Chapter 3	Extended classroom drama: leaning on literature	12
	The Tunnel - Anthony Browne	13
Chapter 4	Drama in literacy time: engaging and reflecting upon text	18
	Mining a text's potential	18
	Selecting drama conventions	19
	Drama and speaking and listening	20
	Drama and reading	21
	Drama and writing	22
Chapter 5	Drama across the curriculum	26
	Drama and history: using the narrative pull of the novel	26
	Drama and geography: using the power of picture books	29
Chapter 6	Planning for drama	32
	Planning extended drama	32
	Mapping out a lesson	33
	Planning role play areas	34
	Final word	37
Appendix	Drama conventions	38
References and bibliography		43

UKLA

The United Kingdom Literacy Association

WITHDRAWN

REVISED EDITION

Drama: Reading, Writing and Speaking Our Way Forward

By Teresa Cremin and Angela Pickard

Minibook 29

UKLA Minibook Series

Series Editor   Eve Bearne
Past Editors   Alison B. Littlefair, Bobbie Neate, Ros Fisher, Susan Ellis

Minibooks in print

Developing Narrative Writing 7-13	Roy Corden
Children's Writing Journals	Lynda Graham and Annette Johnson
Literature Circles: Better Talking, More Ideas	Carole King and Jane Briggs
Making Reading Mean	Vivienne Smith
Storyline - Promoting Language Across the Curriculum	Steve Bell and Sallie Harkness
Miscue Analysis in the Classroom (revised second edition)	Robin Campbell
Classroom Action Research in Literacy: a Guide to Practice	Eve Bearne, Lynda Graham and Jackie Marsh
Active encounters: Inspiring young readers and writers of non-fiction 4-11	Margaret Mallett
Poetry Matters (revised second edition)	Andrew Lambirth
Dyslexia and Inclusion: supporting classroom reading with 7-11 year olds	Rosemary Anderson
Practical Bilingual Strategies for Multilingual Classrooms	Tözün Issa and Alayne Öztürk
Tell Me Another... Speaking, Listening and Learning Through Storytelling	Jacqueline Harrett

Issue number 29
Drama: Reading, Writing and Speaking Our Way Forward
by Teresa Cremin and Angela Pickard

First published 2004 2nd edition 2009   ISBN 978 1 897638 50 7

Published by UKLA
United Kingdom Literacy Association,
4th Floor, Attenborough Building, University of Leicester LE1 7RH   www.ukla.org

Chapter 1

Looking at learning in classroom drama

Drama is both imaginatively engaging and a motivating tool for learning. It encompasses a wide range of practices which involve an act of pretence; these may include work with puppets and props, bringing play scripts to life, small world table top role play, watching and creating theatre, and improvisational classroom drama. The latter involves children in exploring issues in role and improvising alongside their teacher in role, whether in the role play area or in whole class drama. Such drama is often referred to as process drama (Taylor and Warner, 2006), story drama (Booth, 1994) and/or classroom drama (Grainger and Cremin, 2001). Classroom drama, in which the emphasis is on the process not a final theatrical product, is the focus of this book.

Children bring their knowledge, skills, understanding and experience to classroom drama and the teacher's task is to structure and support their enquiries as they inhabit an imaginary world and reflect upon connections between this world and their own. Gradually children also become able to consider the aesthetic formation of their fictional world.

 In classroom drama, teachers guide children's learning journeys through the careful use of different drama conventions, e.g. role play, hot seat, thought tracking, (as detailed in the Appendix). The adroit use of such conventions in extended drama time (see Chapter 3) in literacy time (see Chapter 4), or in cross curricular contexts (see Chapter 5) enables teachers to focus on particular learning areas and ensure progression and continuity. In role play areas too, children can be challenged to learn imaginatively (see Chapter 2), solving problems and creating new ones as they do so. The key to ensuring learning is in the planning (see Chapter 6) and in the lived experience of the drama as teachers make professional decisions based on identified learning areas and the children's interests and ideas.

Through making, performing/sharing, and responding, children learn through drama and about drama and can develop many other skills and competencies. The learning areas particularly pertinent to drama include:

- The development of the whole child
- Language and literacy development
- The development of the imagination
- The content of the drama
- The drama processes
- Reflection.

The development of the whole child

Drama allows children to develop personally and socially in secure imaginative contexts and helps them develop their 'tool box of literacy' (Claxton, 2000). It provides a link between cognitive and affective modes, enabling youngsters to look at contexts in all their complexity and consider their actions and the consequences (Hendy and Toon, 2001). In drama, children make connections between past and present knowledge and experience in order to establish and resolve dilemmas through their active engagement and decision making. Such dilemmas enable children to consider their own values through the 'prism of fiction' (Toye and Prendiville, 2000: 115). In supportive fictional environments, children can develop a richer understanding of themselves as they make sense of the world. This helps them to consider principles that distinguish right from wrong, and develop respect for others, examining issues of truth, equity and justice and the nature of citizenship. Imaginative situations often put children in a position of confronting ethical principles, personal values and moral codes of conduct (Winston, 1998). Opportunities for children to appreciate their own cultural traditions and the diversity and richness of other cultures also exist through drama. Stories from a range of traditions and cultures can be used to develop contexts for drama. Through drama children can also learn to tolerate ambiguity and uncertainty (Grainger, 2003b) and develop their personal and social identities, as drama fosters a sense of community and ownership. Rooted in social interaction, drama is a powerful way to help children relate positively to each other, experience negotiation, and gain confidence and self-esteem.

Language and literacy development

Drama can also make a real contribution to language and literacy development both in the context of literacy based activities and in extended drama time as well as in cross curricular contexts.

Talk is an essential part of the currency of drama. In fictional contexts, authentic reasons to communicate emerge and children are involved in discussing their ideas, generating possible responses in role, co-operating with others and adapting their speech for different purposes and audiences. In this present tense context for literacy learning, they are involved in experimenting with vocabulary and with language styles and registers appropriate to their role and the imaginary situation. The opportunity to reflect upon these choices also contributes to their growing command of the spoken word.

Drama also offers a valuable context for reading; it can be used to 'speak the silence of stories' (Hendy and Toon, 2001:76) and offers learners the chance to actively interrogate texts, exploring and making meaning as they take on roles and look beyond the words themselves. Children can co-author new and living fictions through drama and learn about the nature of reading as they investigate texts in classroom drama (Grainger, 1998).

In addition, the motivating power of drama can provide meaningful contexts for writing, both individually and collaboratively. In-role work can lead to emotive writing from different stances and perspectives and can make a real contribution to children's development as writers (e.g. Barrs and Cork, 2001; Grainger, 2003a, 2003b, 2003c, 2004; Cremin *et al.*, 2006). Children become imaginatively involved in drama and generate ideas for writing through orally rehearsing and refining their views and listening to those of others as they create meaning visually, verbally and kinaesthetically.

The development of the imagination

In drama, children are involved in working imaginatively to improvise and sustain different roles, offering ideas to develop and shape the drama and contributing to the problem solving agenda. In working creatively they construct and inhabit familiar and unfamiliar contexts, and develop credible and coherent alternative worlds in which they encounter the unknown. Children and adults must be prepared to take risks as they move forward together on this journey of discovery. Drama relies heavily upon the imagination and offers real opportunities for its development through the creation of a questioning stance and the exploration of different possibilities and perspectives (Cremin, 2004).

The content of the drama

The content of each drama will relate to an area of the curriculum or life, so it can enable children to develop, use and refine their knowledge and understanding of this area. Drama can make a valuable contribution as children build on their understanding of events, issues or moral dilemmas, enabling them to articulate their voices in a wealth of cross curricular contexts (Toye and Prendiville, 2000; Griffiths, 1991). In investigating issues through drama they will be recognising both influences and turning points in the content frame of the drama and will be able to integrate and employ their factual knowledge with increasing accuracy and understanding.

The drama processes

Through drama children extend their understanding and use of drama skills and conventions to investigate and communicate ideas (see Appendix for an annotated list of conventions). The use of metaphor and symbol, objects or icons that embody meaning in the context, as well as the roles, perspectives and tensions inherent in the situation are all significant components that give drama its challenge, motivation and power. Children are not just drawn to the plot or content, but also to the forms and conventions, which allow them to explore meaning and express their ideas (Neelands, 1998). They learn to select, shape and transform these conventions for themselves and become more adept at discussing the forms, using the drama processes and employing an increasingly critical language to describe and evaluate their drama.

Reflection

Learning in drama arises out of the experience alongside personal and social reflection upon it. There is a constant oscillation between engagement and reflection in drama, and through this process, children develop their reflective capacity and ability to evaluate the drama and make connections to the real world. Gradually their ability to identify and understand parallel situations will develop, as will their ability to recognise patterns and similarities between drama sessions, both in content and in process.

Drama is a rich tool for learning and its progression and development needs to be assessed and recorded. Self-assessment and peer evaluation can enrich teacher assessment in this field and can encourage children to develop a metalanguage to describe drama, enabling them to appreciate and evaluate their own learning. For example, a class may create motionless group sculptures which summarise the key themes in the text and may comment upon each others' interpretations or may discuss the appropriacy of the vocabulary and registers of the roles they adopted. The six areas of learning in drama noted in this chapter need to become the focus of teachers' formative assessment both through in-role observation and participation, and out of role conversation and written reflection. It is also useful to evaluate the children's involvement in the drama session.

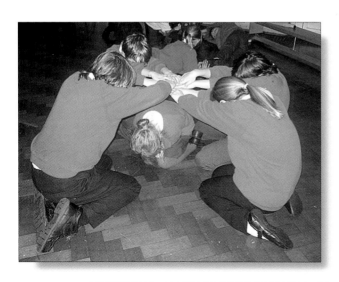

Chapter 2

Drama in role play areas

The imaginary contexts of role play areas enable children to converse, create and draw on their experience, knowledge and understanding of the world to make meaning. In these places they can play out their ideas and investigate characteristics of their culture and the environment. Such opportunities place imagination and innovative thinking at the heart of learning as children manipulate actions and events to create different worlds, and transform themselves and their surroundings (Hendy and Toon, 2001).

Role play areas need to provide a balance between real world contexts, fictional book-based contexts and more generic themes, all of which can become literate contexts in which the children are engaged as speakers, listeners, readers and writers. They may organise and sequence events through oral narratives, employing conventions such as characterisation and may adopt different points of view as they become involved in small group drama. As they do so, they will be expanding their understanding of different settings, making intertextual links and may be involved in reading and writing for different audiences and purposes.

Child initiation and observation

It is essential to provide ample opportunity and time for child-initiated role play, where children can demonstrate their interests, knowledge, and understanding. Observation is fundamental: through listening and watching we can see whether children are stimulated and challenged by their inter-actions with others, with the resources and the context. There are various ways to record such role play, for example, notes, film, tape-recording, taking photographs and engaging the children in recalling events. By observing their serious play, and listening and talking to them while in and out of role, we can evaluate their commitment to, and understanding of, the key learning areas in drama and can also plan, how and where necessary, to intervene in role.

Teacher in role

The unobtrusive presence of an adult enhances play (Singer and Singer, 1990), although, however sensitive, adults can sometimes circumvent children's play in their desire for an identifiable product. We need to decide on an appropriate moment to play alongside children, modelling through role engagement, supporting and challenging their learning (Wood and Attfield, 1996; Cook, 2002). Problematising the play can enrich the children's involvement and commitment and engage them in 'possibility thinking' (Craft, 2000) and in finding solutions in a supportive environment (Bennett *et al*, 1997; Booth, 1994).

Teacher in role (TIR) is a key way to develop the educational potential of role play areas. It involves believing you are someone else, taking on this role and participating with the children. The spontaneous improvisational qualities of such work creates productive tensions, but rather than always adopting high-status roles, adults should try equal or low-status roles as these can create new opportunities. Booth (1994) offers a range of options:

Strategy	Key features
Storyteller	Offers a narrative thread
Leadership	Plays an authority figure and may create conflict
Opposer	Casts disbelief on ideas and challenges
Messenger	Asks for or gives information
Shadow	Acts as a member of a group or community
Low status	Tends to ask for help or assistance

A real life context: a veterinary surgery

This role play area links to work on caring for animals and empathy. Initial preparation might involve discussing children's experiences of vets, a trip to the vets, watching TV programmes such as *Pet Rescue* (Dicovery Animal Planet), websites about animals or a range of fiction involving pets such as Judith Kerr's *Mog and the Ve.Ee.Tt.* (Harper Collins). Resources could include soft toy animals, white/green shirts, medical kits, telephone, appointment diary and keyboard. Language development may relate to social talk, describing symptoms and/or more formal talk, for example, in interviews. The use of non-fiction texts and writing for different purposes such as times of opening, advice on posters, leaflets and noting records of visits can be also developed.

A range of child-initiated pretend play may be observed as children use telephones and discuss and describe symptoms. Children may enjoy being in the role of the receptionist, able to offer or decline an appointment, or value the opportunity to bring their soft toys to see the vet. Indeed the children may want to be in role as the nurse or vet healing the sick animals, running pet care courses and responding to the challenges of working with animals. Activities such as weighing animals, recording symptoms and cures, conducting operations and administering other treatments and medicines may also be carried out. The children may also write prescriptions, such as this one written by a four year old recommending strawberry medicine (Figure 2.1).

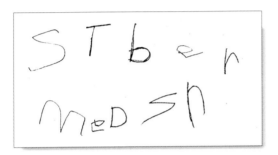

Fig. 2.1: Prescription for strawberry medicine

Teacher in role strategies could involve problems such as the owner who cannot afford to pay their bill, a pet with a ferocious bite who has toothache, a missing pet, a visit from an RSCPA inspector, a leaking gas tap at the surgery, a temporary receptionist who is scared of dogs and so on. Adults could also plan to model different forms of talk and writing.

A fictional setting: *We're Going on a Bear Hunt* - Michael Rosen and Helen Oxenbury (Walker)

This engaging text recounts the journey of a group of children on a bear hunt, and lends itself to the creation of other narratives. To prepare the children you could immerse yourselves in this story and also read *We're going on a Lion Hunt* by David Axtell (Henry Holt) or *Mr Bear and the Bear* by Frances Thomas (Trafalgar Square Books). There are a number of other bear books which would also be relevant to explore different depictions of bears. Resources might include maps, binoculars, equipment and materials that represent the geographical features and a tent to represent the cave. Easy links with geography and science (knowledge and understanding of the world) and indeed PE (physical development) are possible. Children may re-tell the story in role, re-enact the journey to find the bear or they may invent their own versions of the story or parts of it, leaving messages for the bear, taking up roles as other bears moving into the neighbourhood or as children warning the bear about hunters or farmers and so on. Through their play a variety of new characters of all kinds may emerge such as fairies, goblins, skunks and mice entering the fictional frame.

Teacher in role may present a variety of problems and challenges including leaving wanted notices for the bear dead or alive, visiting as a zoo owner who wants to capture the bear, or being a zoologist studying the habitat and feeding patterns of the bear. Writing opportunities (see Figures 2.2. and 2.3) could include modelling a diary of the adventure exploring associated feelings and responses, a message from or to the bear, a list of things to pack for the trip or a local animal newspaper delivered to the cave. The children can also orally re-tell their created stories with you as their scribe. The tent could be used as a holiday base by young people, instead of as a cave, and alternative problems might encompass lost hikers, accidents, noises at night, and missing food which could link the two scenarios.

> "We're going on a tiger hunt. I'll be the poacher. Can I tell you about poachers? I saw it on David Atten (Attenborough) you know, the man on the telly. They have guns and are not very nice people. Did you know that? They hunt animals then they hurt them when they do not have pmissn (permission)"

Fig. 2.2: Sam (4 yrs) Creating his own version of 'We're going on a bear hunt'

> "Don't forget we are pretending not to be scared and at the end the aminal (animal) walks away sad and lonely with no-one there."

Fig 2.3: Sophie (5 yrs) Talking about the image on the inside back cover of 'We're going on a bear hunt'

A generic theme: a time machine

This area is one of infinite possibilities as children can travel to any known or unknown world of their creation, exploring people, places and predicaments from times past, present and future. There are also cross curricular links, particularly in relation to history. In preparation they could watch an excerpt from *Dr. Who* or *The Time Tunnel* by Irwin Allen (20th Century Fox), or visit and respond to fiction texts such as *Mr Benn* by David Mckee (Arrow), the *Magic Key Stories* by Roderick Hunt (Oxford) and *The Time Machine* by H. G Wells. Resources could include cloth and drapes, and/or a large box, fabric or card tunnel, joy sticks, log book, reference texts, access to the internet and maps. Child initiated role play may include the children travelling to different countries, planets, magical places, or times in history and recording their adventures in the log (see Figure 2.4), contacting base via satellite and radio, taking photographs and recording diagrams of places visited and unusual items found. The children could also develop storyboards and write scripts for their role play.

Teacher in Role requires close observation to identify the group's focus and to respond appropriately. It may be possible to use props and artefacts to develop cross curricular links and support their play. Fictional characters could include a travelling wizard, a competing time traveller who wants their time machine, an alien who desires to learn about the human race, or a lost traveller in space who needs to be returned to his own time.

Role play areas can easily lead into whole class drama, for example the class could travel together in a large time machine to meet Florence Nightingale or journey to a planet or the stars; or they could train as veterinary assistants to help out in an epidemic; or camp together on an imaginary school near to the bear's cave. In role play areas and in classroom drama, children can weave together fragments of their own lives, of stories they have heard, seen and read, re-enacting some and creating new narratives through the imagined experience. Improvisation holds sway in such creative contexts as the group creates, investigates and responds to the fictional situation, guided by their teacher who can make full use of different drama conventions to help them.

CAPTAIN'S LOG

05.05.2017

NEW CAPTAIN PREPARING FOR MISSION TO MARVARN

I have taken over as Captain of the starship *Fantasy Traveller*. The ship is my pride and joy. Its weapons and defence systems are the most technically advanced in the fleet and the crew first rate. We have David the Science Oficer, Phillipa is the Medical Officer, Jodi is the Security Officer and Ben is the Engineering Officer.

We are preparing for the mission. We are about to journey to Marvarn. This is an unknown planet. All that is known is that it is bright blue. It is sometimes known as the blue planet and sometimes people think that it is purple.

I'm worried that the mission will do some damage to our weapons and defence systems. We must avoid the black hole.

WEAPONS STRENGTH 12
SHIELDS 18

We have prepared laser pistols for fighting alien creatures.

I will log more news later.

CAPTAIN JAMES

Fig. 2.4: A log entry for 'Time tunnel', James (9 yrs)

Chapter 3

Extended classroom drama: leaning on literature

Drama can empower children to learn actively as they encounter predicaments and seek to solve them in the fictional world of story. In story-drama, as Booth (1994) describes, the narrative provides a powerful hook to prompt the journey of exploration and investigation. However, during the drama you may decide to leave the fictional frame behind and venture into open territory with your class, returning to the structural or thematic support of the text later.

Learning about the story in such contexts occurs through full engagement in the experience which also enables the children to reflect upon the drama, its themes and consequences. O'Neill describes this kind of drama as 'process drama', which 'proceeds without a written script but includes important episodes that will be composed and rehearsed rather than improvised' (O'Neill, 1995: xvi). The children are audience to their own actions and are imaginatively involved in both the creation and consideration of their drama. It is essentially an improvisatory event with an extended timeframe (Heathcote and Bolton, 1995).

Extended whole class drama sessions will encompass a range of conventions, (see Appendix) most notably *Teacher in role*, as the teacher must take a full part in the improvisational encounter. By living inside the text and empathising with the characters, children develop their ability to take roles, identify with others, solve social problems and imagine alternatives; the consequences of which can be examined through the dramatic action. Drama enables children to participate more directly in interpreting and reflecting upon literature and the challenge for teachers is to create access to this fictional world in which they examine the text as both participants and observers.

Examples of such extended drama based on literature can help bring to life its structured yet responsive nature. The example below uses the three stages of a drama session (Grainger and Cremin, 2001), namely, establishing the drama context, introducing conflicts and tensions and drawing the drama together. The activities described as ways into examining the central themes of the book, *The Tunnel* by Anthony Browne (Walker) are not intended to be a lesson plan, but illustrate the possibilities to highlight the variety of drama conventions that can be used to investigate a narrative. You could select from the options however and create a lesson in interaction with your class's interests and ideas.

The Tunnel - Anthony Browne

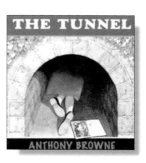

This book is about sibling rivalry and the transformation of a brother-sister relationship. So the *first encounter* with this text needs to highlight the importance of the characters' gender differences, and to investigate this brother-sister relationship in order to establish the dramatic context.

- Read the text up to the point where the brother is scaring his sister. Suggest the children create *small group improvisations* of another occasion in which their gender differences are noticeable; this could be in school, in the park or at home.

- Alternatively, contrasting *freeze frames* (with voice-overs) could be created to show the two children's different daydreams. These might incorporate connections to Browne's use of the fairy tale for the girl or the boy's love of action.

- As you read on, the dilemma of the sister being afraid of the dark could be used to suggest supportive strategies played out in role, as children make connections to their own experiences. Or nightmares could be created through *group sculpture* and *improvisation* and contrasted with the pleasant daydreams explored earlier

- Browne states that the children are always arguing. Their imagined conflicts and arguments could be examined in *pairs role play* or shown through *freeze frames* which focus on gestures, body shapes and facial expression. You might also want to read a variety of poems about gender differences or sibling rivalry at this point to intensify the experience.

- *Roles on the wall* (see Appendix) could be created, one for the girl and one for the boy with comments written outside the role shapes from the perspective of the other sibling.

- Telephone conversations from one of the characters to a friend could explore thoughts and feelings about their sibling, especially if the friend plays devil's advocate and sides with the sibling (See Figure 3.1).

'Hello Kelly'

'Hi Rose what's up?'

'Oh it's my brother again'

'What's he done this time?'

'The usual, scaring me he's wearing a mask now pretending he's from a horror movie. I'm having nightmares!'

'Tell your mum'

'I have but she thinks we're as bad as each other and just tells him to stop. He says I'm imagining it. I hate him sometimes!'

Fig 3.1: Example of a telephone conversation

As the drama develops, *conflicts and tensions* come to the fore. Read on to where the brother decides that he is going inside the mysterious tunnel; the activities in this stage of the drama will open up the imaginary world.

- Explore the sister's feelings through a *decision alley* (see Appendix), identifying the advantages and disadvantages of following her brother into the dark tunnel. Or ask the class to stand in position, posing as the sister peering into the tunnel, and engage in interior monologue - thinking out loud - what should she do, whom should she tell, should she call out or follow him, would he come after her ...?

- You could adopt mum's role back at home, and as *Teacher in role* voice aloud your thoughts, revealing your concerns about the lateness of your children. Or ask one child to join you and show the class the telephone conversation between mum and dad as they reflect upon the absence of their children. This could also be undertaken in pairs.

- As the tension builds, the sister decides to go into tunnel. The children could close their eyes and visualise the place with you describing her fears, which are fuelled by her knowledge of fairy tales.

- As she emerges into the wood, then a dark forest, invite the class to join you in creating the place. Use the powerful pictures to create the threatening scene with children in groups, pairs and on their own becoming figures of threat and fear. Noises, using body percussion or instruments, could also be added to create atmosphere and one child in role could walk through this apparent forest of doom with the trees, goblins, sprites, woodcutters and so on whispering words that spin terror into her heart. You might also suggest that hidden within the wood were good spirits or figures who want to encourage the girl and who offer words of support.

- As this is happening, enter in role as the wicked stepmother looking for Snow White's cottage. You represent another threat at this point and can enquire where the girl is heading; you might decry her need to find her brother, and suggest she returns home to safety. Alternatively, ask the class to adopt the role of the girl, and, as the stepmother, try to persuade them that they would be better to return home. Remind them of the dangers of the forest and of their brother's different behaviour. You could suggest you have watched them through your magic mirror.

In the *resolutions* phase of the drama, when the meanings are drawn together, you may want to explore the discovery of her brother, the girl's literal and symbolic embrace of him and later the transformation in their relationship.

- Narrate the departure of the stepmother and the confused state of the girl, and then ask the class to make a circle around one boy. Share the illustration of the boy turned to stone and invite the boy to adopt the position indicated by Browne. Now she has found him, what is she thinking? Ask them to suggest ideas to one another in preparation for this *thought tracking*, and encourage them to step forward in role and voice their thoughts.

- The child in role as the boy in the middle might also be invited to respond to these thoughts or voice his own thoughts.

- Having shown the hug, and read to the end of the text, invite the children in small groups to create *group statues* that reflect the theme of the text, without using the actual characters. Perhaps one of the siblings made this in art at school, what might it be made of and where might it be placed in the home? What might it be called?

- The convention *flashforward* could be used to reflect their relationship some six months later, with small groups creating *improvisations* of a telling future incident. This may leave the text open and reflect the complexity of living.

Such extended classroom drama could also involve diary or letter writing (See Figure 3.2). The poems read during the drama could be re-examined,

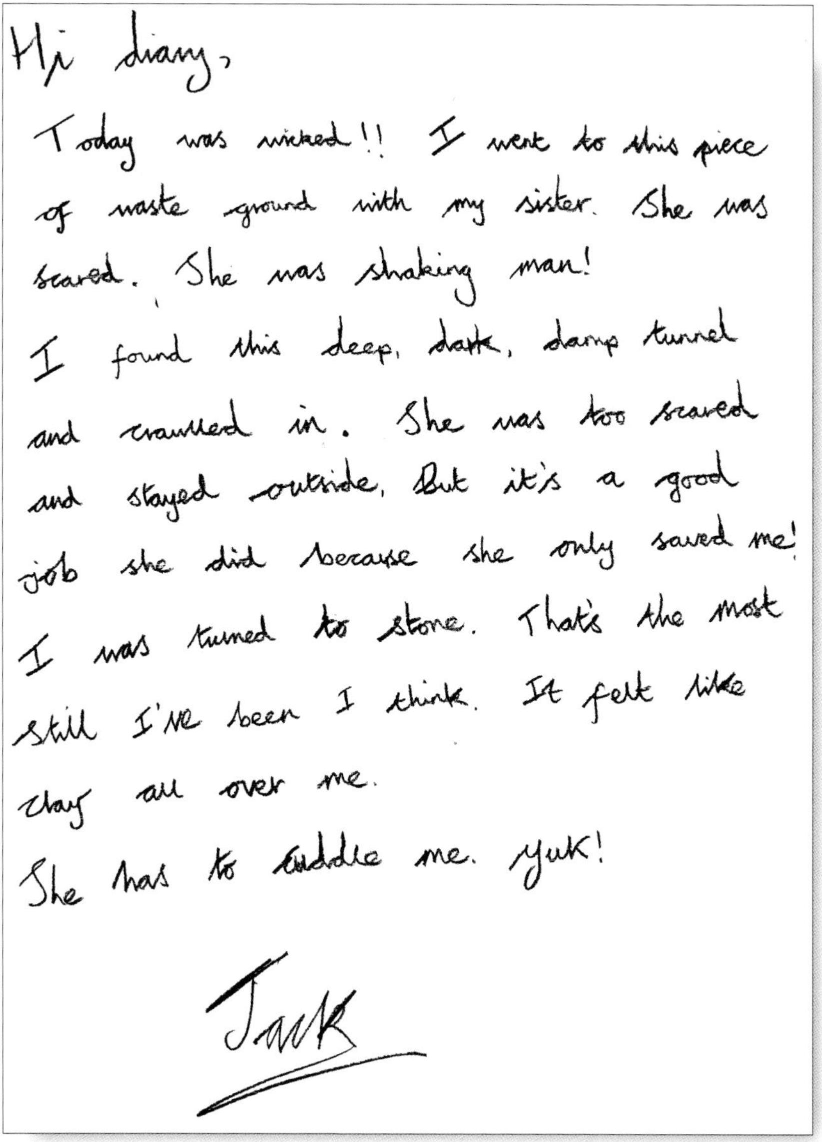

Hi diary,

Today was wicked!! I went to this piece of waste ground with my sister. She was scared. She was shaking man!

I found this deep, dark, damp tunnel and crawled in. She was too scared and stayed outside. But it's a good job she did because she only saved me! I was turned to stone. That's the most still I've been I think. It felt like clay all over me.

She had to cuddle me. Yuk!

Jack

Fig 3.2: Diary entry by boy, age 10 years.

and the children's own sibling relationships or friendships could be discussed. Through creating and inhabiting imaginary worlds in this way with their teacher, and reflecting upon them during the drama and after the action, children can learn about much themselves and their own world.

Chapter 4

Drama in literacy time: engaging and reflecting upon text

Classroom drama can play a motivating and enriching role in literacy time, since it fosters the interdependence of the language modes and enables engagement and reflection upon text. Drama conventions can be flexibly employed to investigate and explore the content, construction and authorial stance of fiction and non-fiction texts. Improvisation prompts children's full participation and involvement, and can, in particular, develop their understanding of characters, theme and language. Drama activities need, however, to be fully embedded within the elements of literacy time and not used as 'warm up' tasks merely to motivate the children. This is to underestimate the potential of drama to provide imaginary contexts in which reading, writing and speaking and listening are a natural response.

In placing children in both formal and informal fictional situations, drama facilitates oral involvement in a range of registers, encourages a closer examination of the text being studied, and offers authentic opportunities for purposeful writing. Through increasing both the teacher's and the children's involvement in the issue or theme, drama can help the class dig down into the substrata of the text.

Mining a text's potential

In selecting a moment from a literary or non-fiction text to expand through a drama convention, it is important to choose carefully and consider its suitability as a dramatic prompt. Questions worth considering include:

- Does the class know enough of the characters / story / setting to, for example, project imaginatively forwards or backwards in the text?

- What possible 'offstage' scenarios might be occurring that could be fruitfully investigated?

- What possible roles or conventions could be employed at this moment and with what specific purpose?

- How much needs to be read aloud immediately before the drama to contextualise the action?

Tension is a critical element in drama, so moments need to be selected which focus on conflict, ambiguity, challenge or misunderstanding. These will help trigger more focused improvisations, and will draw the children imaginatively into the situations in which the characters find themselves. Fiction is full of unresolved conflicts to choose from and non-fiction too examines contested issues, enabling children to encounter and resolve predicaments of various kinds. Some tensions are self evident in the context of a text, for example, in *Angry Arthur* by Hiawayn Oram (Picture Puffin), Arthur wants to stay up and watch TV, but his mother refuses. Other tensions can be found through examining gaps in the text, perhaps unmentioned conversations, nightmares, premonitions, a character's conflicting thoughts on an issue, or earlier problematic events that hint at the challenge to come. Through drama, these 'omissions' can be constructed, investigated and packed with meaning.

Without experiencing a genuine sense of conflict or difficulty through engagement in role and in response to the fictional situations encountered, there would be no drama. So you need to dig down into a rich textual seam, selecting or creating a significant moment of tension in the text to investigate further. If shared writing follows the dramatic improvisation then this can be used for teaching about conventions of the text, sentence and word level features, so the potential of the moment is important not only in relation to the drama but also be in relation to text production opportunities.

Selecting drama conventions

A plethora of drama conventions can be harnessed to aid the comprehension and composition of texts. These are tools for investigating meaning and represent a palette of choices that can be flexibly used to frame and focus an investigation in the context of the text (Neelands, 1998). So, in addition to selecting a potentially rich and tense moment in a text, you need to identify the most appropriate convention to serve your purpose. If you want to establish further information about a character for example, then conventions such as *hot seating* (when a person in role is asked questions by others), *thought tracking, decision alley, role on the wall* and *writing in role* may be useful (see Appendix). To focus on story structure however, the conventions *freeze frame, forum theatre* (see Appendix) or *storytelling* may be more suitable. Each also provokes particular kinds of talk and writing, which may influence selection.

Drama and speaking and listening

Elements of speaking and listening in schools often include: speaking, listening, group discussion and interaction and drama. If drama is well planned and developed, then all four elements can be encompassed through quality drama provision. For example in *George Speaks* by Dick King Smith (Puffin), we are introduced to baby George, who reveals his remarkable ability to speak fluently to his sister, Laura. Concerned to ensure he does not become a prodigy, George insists Laura tells no-one. Together however, they seize opportunities to talk and are often caught in challenging situations where secrecy is important. Selecting one of these, role play in pairs can help the children generate possible conversations between George and Laura. The *Teacher in role* as one of their parents could also intervene, adding further tension and challenge and confronting the whole class. The children will be generating conversations, asking and answering questions, retelling events and hypothesising and enacting new ones in pairs or small groups.

Alternatively, in *Bad Girls* by Jacqueline Wilson (Corgi Yearling), a telephone conversation between Tanya and Mandy could be role played in pairs, for example, when Tanya seeks to persuade Mandy to go shoplifting with her. The oral language in this context will be quite different, encompassing persuasive talk, the language of peer pressure, cajoling and defending. This *role play* could also be undertaken with half the class as Mandy, and half as Tanya, which enables the ideas generated in pairs to be shared in the wider forum.

In non-fiction work, discursive texts can be brought to life through the convention *decision alley*, which is excellent for representing arguments for and against a particular subject. Two lines of children face one another, each side representing one viewpoint and voicing the pros or cons of, for example, extending the school day. The advantages and disadvantages can be summarised and used for discursive writing or written as speech bubbles for a display. Alternatively, *small group improvisation* of a radio or TV advert accompanied by the posters and handbills which are part of a persuasive advertising campaign can be created. Viewing or listening to adverts and identifying their persuasive features will sharpen these productions, which may be mini-narratives or encompass song, dance, music, PowerPoint™ or recommendations from 'experts'. You can evaluate these together for their persuasive capacity and the features of the presentation that tempted the customers to buy the object or to go to see the show.

Drama and reading

Through making full use of drama conventions, teachers can help children explore and develop their inferential understanding about texts and become more effective at reading both text and subtext. By selecting particular moments in texts and exploring these through drama, children can make deductions and connections to their current knowledge, for example about the narrative or the issues in a non-fiction text. They can also extend their understanding of characters' motives, behaviour and possible histories. In drama, an 'aesthetic' reading of the text is created, in which the focus is on the insights and satisfaction gained from the textual encounter (Rosenblatt, 1978). On the drama journey the children will be involved in a variety of processes that are central to both reading and drama, including:

- predicting
- constructing images
- making imaginative connections
- co-authoring
- developing empathy
- engaging emotionally
- reflecting.
  (Grainger, 1998:35).

In shared reading, drama is a particularly powerful tool to reveal more about characters, narrative events and key themes. For example, in *Where's My Teddy* by Jez Alborough (Walker), *thinking out loud in role* as one of the main characters can help generate insights about the great big bear and poor Eddie, both of whom lose their teddies. Adopting physical positions similar to the characters at significant moments in the tale and voicing their thoughts can support both inference and deduction skills.

Drama can also help children read both the word and the world (Freire, 1985) through the adoption of multiple viewpoints and the examination of context, text and subtext. In non- fiction, a living timeline with *freeze frames* of significant events in particular period can be made. Initially groups identify significant moments or events in, for example, World War II and then make freeze frames of them. Once subtitles have been added, these can be ordered chronologically, perhaps adding others to ensure coverage. This can be undertaken at the start of a project to ascertain what the class already know about, for example, events in the Victorian era, or can reflect their learning at the end of a period of study. Each group could also write a brief paragraph recounting their event, which could be joined to other recounts in shared writing; or newspaper reports could be created.

Drama and writing

Drama can act as a valuable precursor to writing and encourages ideas about the text to be spun into existence, with alternative perspectives voiced in role and new insights about the text uncovered (Cremin *et al.*, 2006). For example, in *The Wreck of the Zanzibar* by Michael Morpurgo (Mammoth), the family is devastated when young Billy leaves home. Laura could be hot seated by her friends or family to find out her views on his departure and her conjectures about his reasons for leaving. Later, members of her family might think out loud in *interior monologues* pondering the situation, which could lead to diary or letter writing from their various perspectives.

In non-fiction, *small group improvisations* in the style of presenters on children's programmes such as *Blue Peter* or *Art Attack* can enable the structure and purpose of instructions in televisual contexts to be examined. It is worth watching a couple of examples of such programmes with the class first, drawing connections to written instructions, discussing options and allowing preparation time. Groups could even use their own art and craft work. Class 'dress rehearsals' and a semi-formal television 'viewing' session may help and written instructions can be produced for the programme's website (see Figure 4.1). Alternatively, the *Teacher in role* as cookery programme presenter Jamie Oliver, for example, can show how to prepare a recipe on which the class can make notes and then write up the instructions for a BBC recipe leaflet. These are both useful activities to gauge what the children know about the structure, organisation and language features of procedural texts. For additional ideas see Grainger *et al.* (2004) for fiction and non-fiction texts.

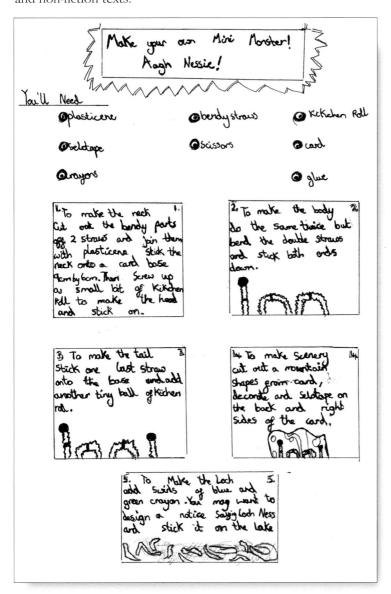

Fig. 4.1: Instructional writing: Make your own mini monster

Different text types can usefully be connected to drama conventions as the list in Figure 4.2 indicates, although teachers will make their own links to suit their particular purposes in writing.

Right; Figure 4. 2 Drama conventions for different text types

Recount	• Storytelling in role • Series of freeze frames with voice over • TV interview recounting an event • *This is Your Life* improvisation • Eye witnesses work
Diary	• Thought tracking • Telephone conversation
Report	• Freeze frame • Hot seating
Poetry	• Group sculpture on theme • Ritual
Instructions	• Group improvisation • Freeze frames of process
Story structure	• Freeze frame significant events as storyboard • Improvised flashback / flashforward • Forum theatre • Oral retelling in role
Explanation	• Documentary improvisation
Dialogues	• Role play • Thought tracking • Interior monologue
Notes/minutes	• Hot seating in role • Formal meeting • Role play
Persuasive/discursive	• Decision alley • Collective voice • Formal meeting
Advertisement	• Group improvisation
Playscript	• Role play in pairs/groups • Small group play making

25

Chapter 5

Drama across the curriculum

Drama can make a valuable contribution to children's learning in cross curricular contexts. In imaginative worlds, children find themselves using and extending their mathematical, scientific, linguistic, historical and geographical knowledge, as well as using their skills and understanding. In humanities contexts for example, children often identify questions for investigation, and areas of interest that can be explored through drama enabling them to 'learn through imagined experience' (Neelands, 1992). Drama can transform their partial knowledge and help them hold information up to scrutiny.

Fiction has a significant role to play in this process, since it can build effective bridges with characters, situations, problems and themes, personalising the arena and enabling both connections and understanding to be developed. In fiction, tension and conflict play a central role; these are also concepts central to drama, so framing cross curricular explorations in the context of children's literature or faith stories can markedly enrich the drama created.

Drama and history: using the narrative pull of the novel

Through drama, children can revisit the narratives of the past, examine parallel issues in the present, and look to the future with new understanding. Combining fiction and drama can make the past more accessible, and develop children's insight and empathetic understanding. Drama often generates as many questions as it answers, and provokes the desire to find out, enabling the use and application of historical knowledge.

Historical novels in particular help to populate the period with living characters and encourage the examination of genuine conflicts. The politics and living conditions of the time, as well as social and economic practices, can be investigated through the imagined experience of the characters. Re-enactment of a known narrative is not sought, but scenes or gaps can be improvised so a variety of perspectives are examined in the context of extended classroom drama. In *Children of Winter* by Berlie Doherty for example, Catherine and her two younger siblings are taken to a safe haven outside the village of Eyam during the plague or 1665-1666. They survive with difficulty, not fully understanding their isolation and prevented even from hugging their mother when she comes to visit. Their dilemma, and the accounts of the plague, can be fleshed out through role play, thought tracking, decision alleys and other conventions; and diaries, notes or letters can be written. Children could close such projects by producing a television documentary about the area of focus, making full use of primary evidence, and with first-hand imagined accounts written in role.

Historical novels can be used in classroom drama, both in the context of extended drama and in briefer dramatic encounters in the context of history time. The possibilities include:

- *Co-authoring a new chapter:* during the reading of the novel and the related study of the period, create another possible chapter. Use *flashbacks* or *flash forwards* and involve the children in creating *group freeze frames* or *improvisations* of an earlier or later event in the tale/period.

- *Relying on a chapter to guide the drama:* select a chapter, and read up to this point and then let the narrative guide you forwards. Read and stop intermittently, inviting the children to suggest ways of finding out more about the characters, their situation or the period. Take up their ideas and together enrich the language of the unsaid by involving them in *improvisations* using different drama conventions.

- *Co-authoring a follow up tale:* read the novel, finish your study of the period, and then explore the long-term consequences for one of the characters. By exploring ways in which the past might shape characters' fictional futures, you'll be able to ascertain what the children have learned.

Various texts can support the imaginative reconstruction and examination of history. Recommendations include:

Significant people

The Boy Who Sailed with Columbus by Michael Foreman (Pavilion)
Sir Francis Drake by Roy Gerrard (Gollanz)
King Henry VIII's Shoes by Karen Wallace (Collins)
I had a Dream by Dr Martin Luther King, Jr (Dial)
Stone Girl, Bone Girl by Laurence Anholt (Mary Anning)
The Last Wolf by Michael Morpurgo (Bonnie Prince Charlie) (Heinemann)
My Friend Walter by Michael Morpurgo (Sir Walter Raleigh) (Heinemann)

The Egyptians

The Dream Master by Theresa Breslin (Puffin)
Croc O'Nile by Roy Gerrard (Gollanz)
I am the Mummy Herb Nefert by Eve Bunting (Voyager)

The Plague

A Parcel of Patterns by Jill Paton Walsh (Collins)
Children of Winter by Berlie Doherty (Puffin)

Victorian England

Fair's Fair by Leon Garfield (Simon and Schuster)
Street Child by Berlie Doherty (Bodley Head)
Lady Daisy by Dick King Smith (Puffin)
My Granny was a Buffer Girl by Berlie Doherty (Hodder Headline)
Coram Boy by Jamila Gavin (Egmont)

World War II

Rose Blanche retold by Ian McKewan (Jonathon Cape)
Johnnie's Blitz by Bernard Ashley (Puffin)
A Long Way Home by Ann Turnbull (Walker)
The Machine Gunners by Robert Westall (Macmillan)
A Country Childhood: War Boy by Michael Foreman (Pavilion)

First and second hand evidence can also be used to trigger or enhance historical drama, such as facsimiles of old documents, physical artefacts, paintings and photographs.

Drama and geography: using the power of picture books

In geography, a focus on place can highlight the human and economic issues that will help charge the drama, and this sense of place can be offered through quality picture fiction. The visuals will prompt questions to investigate and the drama will help shape understanding of complexity and compromise. Local environmental issues, such as the placement of airports or shopping centres, the reduction in green belt, and the use of insecticides can all be investigated through drama. Again, the power and potency of photographs, news articles and related picture fiction can help to make the issues relevant and facilitate the development of informed views, not just apparent surface knowledge.

The strong predicaments and the images in picture fiction draw the reader into the fictional world. For example, in a drama on the rainforest, the picture book *The Great Kapok Tree: A Tale of the Amazonian Rainforest* by Lynne Cherry (Harcourt Brace) can help the imaginative creation of the homes and habitats of the Huaroni. The forest atmosphere could be contrasted with the noise of the Rio slums through *sound tracking* and meetings between financiers, surveyors, tribes-folk and governments can all be improvised. *Writing in role* may include: letters, news items, aid workers' reports, articles in environmental magazines. Such authentic writing in a fictional world frame can build on the children's existing knowledge and will often lead to a more motivated examination of the available information (See Figure 5.1 overleaf).

Picture books can be used in different ways to stimulate dramatic inquiry in geography and other areas of learning. These include:

- *Children creating their own tale based on the opening scenario and visuals:* after reading and sharing the pictures from the first part of the text, move into drama mode. Improvise the remainder of the text, examining previous and future action and retaining a focus on the theme and the nature and consequences of human involvement.

- *Prefiguring the text through drama:* identify the key theme of the chosen book, and develop a drama around this prior to reading it. In effect the drama investigation is an analogy for the text.

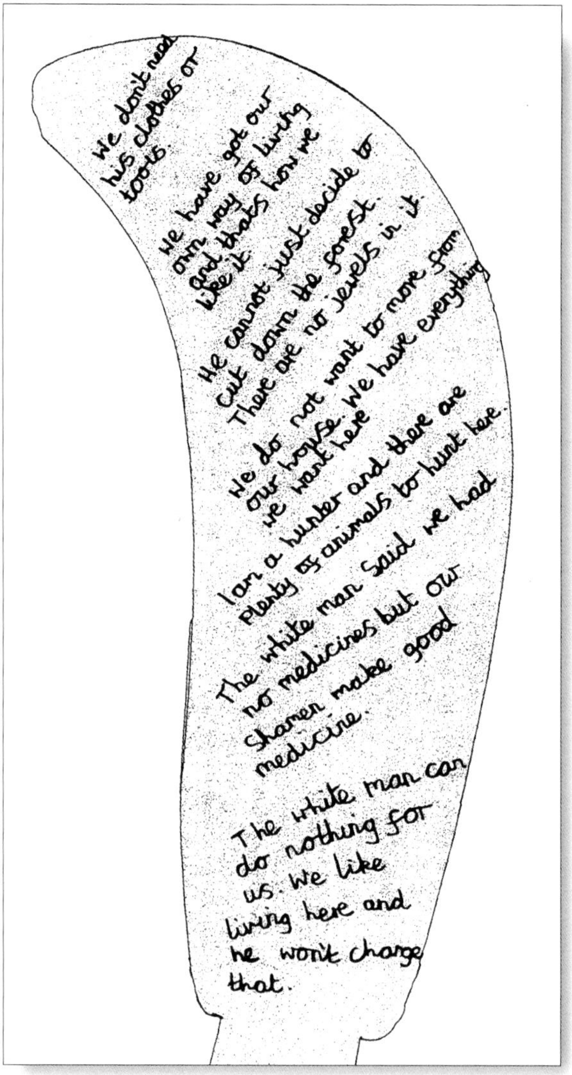

Fig. 5.1: Child's writing in role as the inhabitant of a threatened rain forest

We don't need his clothes or tools. He have got our own way of living and thats how we like it. He cannot just decide to cut down the forest. There are no jewels in it. He do not want to more scam our house. We have everything we want here. I am a hunter and there are plenty of animals to hunt here. The white man said we had no medicines but our shamen make good medicine. The white man can do nothing for us. We like living here and he won't change that.

- *Taking the picture book as your guide:* share the tale in stages, preferably using visuals in the IWB, stopping intermittently to allow the children to inhabit the gaps in meaning left by the text. The tale will shape and guide the drama and re-enactment is avoided.

Recommended picture books for examining geographical issues include:

Window by Jeannie Baker (Red Fox)
The Great Kapok Tree by Lynne Cherry (Harcourt Brace)

The Trouble with Thunder Mountain by Russell Hoban (Penguin)
Shaker Lane by Alice and Martin Provensen (Walker)
Aunty Dot's Atlas by Eljay Yildrim (Collins)
The Magic Bicycle by Brian Patten (Walker)
Giant by Juliet and Charles Snape (Walker)
The Day of Ahmed's Secret by Florence Parry Heide (Gollanz)
The Paperbag Prince by Colin Thompson (Red Fox)

Cross curricular drama is strengthened through the use of quality fiction as a frame for action and investigation; it may be spread over several weeks or may be a single session, but its potential to contribute to children's learning across the curriculum can be tapped by allowing the fictive world of literature to enliven the focus, and help children personalise and connect to the area of study. Faith tales too can be explored from the inside out, enabling children to deepen their understanding of particular religions and the significant people within them. Social and moral opportunities abound in these contexts, as well as spiritual ones, through which children increase their self-knowledge, and search for meaning and purpose in life (Winston,1998; Grainger and Kendall-Seatter, 2003). The literature selected becomes a guide for developing imagination in action and a context for knowledge expansion.

Chapter 6

Planning for drama

Drama involves us in being other people in other places with problems to solve. So in terms of planning drama, we need to identify these crucial elements prior to the sessions, although on many occasions additional predicaments will arise from the children's imaginative involvement. Similarly, in the context of the role play area, people, place and predicament are central planning tools, and opportunities for learning can be capitalised upon as a consequence of observing the children's involvement.

Planning extended drama

In extended drama we need to retain a balance between the planned structure or intention of the session, and the children's interests which will shape and evolve during the fictional encounter. A wealth of resources can help us plan, and fiction in particular is a supportive structure, since it offers a fictional frame for us as professionals to build upon. Working with the class, we can identify gaps in the text and investigate these through drama, or the text can be used to springboard into drama creating a new chapter or tale, since drama seeks to examine the situations and tensions, themes and characters within the narrative.

Drama sessions often operate seamlessly, but in fact can usefully be divided up into three major sections.

- *First encounters:* creating the drama context. This involves introducing and establishing the narrative elements of people, place and predicament with the class.

- *Conflicts and tensions:* developing the drama. This involves focusing upon and investigating the major dramatic tension and learning areas.

• **Resolutions:** drawing the drama together. This involves harnessing the children's ideas and insights, shaping the culmination to the fiction and reflecting on learning (Grainger and Cremin, 2001).

The plan of the lesson should enable us to feel secure since an overall structure is in place and whilst the children's reactions and ideas cannot be predicted, the shape provides a flexible framework for the dramatic investigation.

Mapping out a lesson

A. Initially the teacher needs to identify the *main* focus. This is the connecting curriculum thread, e.g. a focus on the Egyptians; people from the past; or stories focused upon bullying.

B. From this the *teaching phases and objectives* can be created. These may be chosen/adapted from banks of objectives (e.g. Primary National Strategy, 1998/2006; Bunyan *et al*, 2000) but should relate to two or three of the learning areas in drama which include: the development of the whole child; the imagination; language and literacy; the content of the drama; the drama processes; and reflection (See Chapter 1). In a drama based around Florence Nightingale for example, it may be appropriate to focus on the historical content and the drama processes if new conventions are being introduced. This is not to suggest that the children will not be using their imaginations and developing their use of language in these sessions, but that the teaching objectives need to be focused, feasible and appropriate.

C. *Identify the people, place and predicament.* This is the essence of the drama around which individual sessions can be planned; teachers can invent these narrative elements or can turn to the diverse world of fiction and borrow elements from this. In addition, visuals of many kinds can be used: paintings and sculptures, photographs and comic strips, as well as single illustrations from picture books or poetry collections. For example, Charles Keeping's evocative visuals in *Beowulf* and *The Lady of Shallot* (Oxford) are valuable resources even if these stories themselves are not being explored. Alternatively, poems, which hint at a predicament or describe a setting in detail, can be used. You may choose to use the actual resource in the drama or you can develop the drama around the resource yourself and share it during the drama session or at the end.

The people, the place and the problem can be identified from the resource, or just one of these elements can be borrowed and the remainder invented by the teacher and children. The imaginative choices we make at this stage and the way in which we involve the class will have a marked influence on the drama. As Bruner (1986) suggests:

> *We know the world in different ways, from different stances, and each of the ways in which we know it produces different structures or representations, or indeed 'realities'... we become increasingly adept at seeing the same set of events from multiple perspectives or stances and at entertaining the results as, so to speak, alternative possible worlds.* (Bruner, 1986:109)

D. *Planning the actual drama session* will involve the teacher in identifying appropriate drama conventions to both create and reflect upon the drama context. In first encounters, initial strategies need to be chosen that open intriguing doors into the drama world and entice the learners in, helping them build belief in the drama. Avoid lengthy conversations and get the action going as soon as possible, perhaps through teacher in role or narration moving the action on after an initial role-play or freeze frame. You could make use of the resource and lean on the literature to help you create the fictional world and develop a sense of who they are in this context.

In the *conflicts and tensions stage* as the drama unfolds you will need to keep up the pace, variety and value of the conventions employed to explore the central predicament. This will deepen the children's involvement and will help them raise issues and questions to investigate. In this stage the class will move in and out of the drama, oscillating between engagement and reflection. In the *final resolutions stage* the drama will gradually be drawn together through your use of more reflective conventions and will seize the opportunities you provide to consider their learning.

Planning role play areas

In these areas, children need to be able to draw on real and vicarious experiences and their knowledge and understanding of the world, so the setting (place), the characters (people), and their problems (predicaments) are also important here. A balance of child initiated and teacher initiated opportunities for learning will need to be planned. This may involve the placing of problems in an area, for example, a note left in the café explaining that the chef is ill but there is a children's party booked for that day. It is of paramount importance though, that we support the authenticity of children's ideas and feel relaxed with what can appear to be, to adults, somewhat messy and haphazard. Teacher initiated opportunities may be based upon observation and responsive intervention to capitalise on the potential for learning.

There are a number of ways teachers can plan for a range of opportunities:

A. *Identify the main focus* which may be related to real life, such as a hospital or supermarket, or it could be connected to well known fiction, such as the bear's cave from *We're Going on a Bear Hunt* by Michael Rosen (Simon & Schuster) or Mrs Wobble the Waitresses' cafe from Alan Ahlberg's *Happy Families* collection (Puffin). Alternatively, it could be a more generic imaginary setting such as the moon, a cottage in a wood, the ocean or a magic garden. Popular culture examples can also work well such as *In the Night Garden* (BBC/Ragdoll), *Bob the Builder's workshop* (Hit entertainment plc) or *Fireman Sam's* fire station (BBC Worldwide). By providing different kinds of environment the children will have the opportunity to explore a range of different situations. When deciding on the theme, make connections to a key area of learning such as the Communication, Language and Literacy area of the Birth to Five /Foundation Stage Curriculum in England or a part of an area of study from the National Curriculum such as 'Growth' or 'Materials'.

B. *Prepare together and build on the children's interests*. A visit to a real life place can enrich the children's knowledge and understanding. Guest speakers too can be invited in to discuss their work in such places, and for fiction-based role play immersion in the main book and related texts and TV programmes can help support the children's play. The children also need to be involved in resourcing the imaginative and physical aspects of the area.

C. *Resource the area for imaginative play: the people, place and predicaments.* The children can be involved in generating lists of possible people who might, for example, work in or visit the garden centre or enchanted forest. Then in twos they can try out such roles, being the complaining customer or the lost fairy asking for help from a goblin. This might be modelled for them first. Their brainstorms could be accompanied by pictures or posters of wanted criminals, job adverts or photographs in the doctor's surgery of people who work there. Possible problems that might be encountered in these places could also be pooled and listed, e.g. water leaks, power cuts, inspectors' visits, burglaries, complaining customers, lost children and so on. These will be tailored to the area and the age of the children involved.

The intention is not to limit or direct the role play but to assist the children in engaging in imaginative play through becoming aware of possible roles and predicaments. Such lists also support us as busy teachers in identifying possible *Teacher in role* scenarios with which to enter the area and extend the children's imaginary play. Predicaments can also be seeded in written form. For example, a hidden message from Friar Tuck warning of an ambush, an invitation to a party, a note about one of the animals being ill.

D. *Resource the area for literate role play.* When making decisions in relation to appropriate props and resources for the area, it is important to consider a cultural mix and have an awareness of gender bias. The provision of books, notepads, maps, reference texts, paper for lists, memos, diaries, log books, notice boards and so on, as appropriate to the area, will enable teacher intervention to support writing in particular genres. The children will also find their own reasons for writing, leaving codes, making lists of appointments, menus, diagrams etc. especially if this has been modelled, introduced or is needed for a particular imaginative purpose within their play.

E. Select relevant *teaching objectives* related to the areas of learning in drama. With careful adult observation and intervention these can be targeted and achieved. For example, through intervening in role as a lost mermaid, the teacher may help a group focus and prompt more purposeful use of language and literacy by challenging the group to tell stories about their part of the ocean or encouraging them to produce a map. On some occasions, however, the children's role play may be observed, and their playful learning recorded without intervention or the use of specified objectives.

Final word

Drama is a potent tool in supporting young learners as they read, write, talk and imagine their way forwards. Its motivating power supports both teachers and children as they take risks, create new and imaginary worlds and learn from living in these worlds together.

Appendix

Drama conventions

Each drama convention creates different demands and prompts particular kinds of thinking and interaction at key points in the drama. Conventions work best if there is some element of ambiguity, uncertainty or tension inherent in the fictional scenario. They are not rigid structures but can be combined and adapted to suit the dramatic exploration. Brief preparation time before each convention is often helpful in generating ideas, so the children are not pressured to take part in a hot seat for example before they have had the chance to think out possible questions with a partner.

Decision alley

This is useful to examine conflicting interests or dilemmas and reveals the pros and cons of a particular decision. Two lines of children face each other and one child in role as a character walks slowly down the alley between them. As they progress, their thoughts or the sets of views for and against a particular course of action are voiced aloud by the rest of the class standing in the two lines. The character can be hot seated at the end of the alley, to ascertain their decision and its justification.

Drawing

This involves children individually or in small groups drawing a significant object in the drama. For example, a detailed drawing of flora and fauna found during the migration west of the American pioneers may help children invent possibilities and sow seeds for future action. The drawing enhances the drama and creates new meanings.

Forum theatre

This is an improvisation performed by a few members of the class in the forum of the classroom, which then is discussed, revisited and developed. In its simplest form, an important situation is improvised and watched by the class, and the words and actions of those involved are commented upon (with the helpful mediation of the teacher) and then the same situation is reworked taking into account what has been said. A development of this technique is to offer the children, actors or observers, the chance to stop the action, suggest changes and justify their alternative ideas. It is most useful in a tense or significant situation.

Freeze frame

This convention is also known as creating tableaux, still images or making statues. Individually, in small groups or as a whole class, the children use their bodies to create an image of an event, an idea, a theme or a moment in time. This silent picture freezes the action, as do newspaper pictures, but it can also portray a memory, a wish, or an image from a dream, as well as represent abstract themes such as anger, jealousy or the truth. Freeze frames can be brought to life, and subtitled with appropriate captions, written or spoken, and may have noises and sound effects added to them. In addition, the words or inner thoughts of members of the tableau can be voiced when the teacher touches children on the shoulder. Freeze frames offer a useful way of capturing and conveying meaning, since groups can convey much more than they would be able to through words alone.

Hot seating

The teacher and/or a small group of children assume the role of one or more individuals from the drama and are questioned by the remainder of the class, who are also in role. The class need to be forewarned and primed to think of questions. This is a useful probing technique which seeks to develop knowledge of a character's motives, attitudes and behaviour and increases awareness of the complex nature of human behaviour.

Improvisation: small group

Improvisations can be prepared beforehand or spontaneously developed. In small groups, children discuss, plan and create a piece of prepared improvisation which is relatively secure, because they will have discussed a kind of script or structure to follow. In spontaneous improvisation, the group let the action unfold as they bring the situation into existence.

Improvisation: whole class

The whole class, including the teacher in role, improvise together. It can be planned or spontaneous, 'formal', e.g. a court scene, or informal, e.g. a market scene. Whole class role play reduces the pressure of being watched since everyone is corporately engaged and lives inside the moment, responding to each other spontaneously within the imaginary context. Roles are adopted prior to the improvisation and benefit from being discussed.

Mantle of the expert

This involves children being given, or adopting roles, which necessarily include the expertise, authority, knowledge and skills of specialists. This knowledge may be recently acquired from classroom research, or may be bestowed imaginatively by the teacher in role, welcoming them as e.g. nurses or scientists. The status it gives the children, allows them to significantly influence the drama. The teacher honours their expertise and ensures they can use it in the drama.

Overheard conversations

In small groups, conversations between characters are improvised, and a few 'overheard' by the class. This adds tension, offers information and enables a range of viewpoints to be heard. Key conversations from the past can also be created. The teacher as storyteller may later integrate these perspectives into the drama.

Ritual or ceremony

The teacher and the class create some form of ceremony, which is part of the drama, to work out ways of marking significant events in the narrative. This slows the drama down and provokes a deepening sense of significance as well as reflection. For example, children as villagers might create a chant, a prayer or a dance to thank the gods for their beneficence. Ritual is often used to conclude work or to intensify the emotional tenor of the drama.

Role on the wall

An outline is drawn around an important character as they lie upon a large piece of paper. Information and feelings about the character are written into the shape by each child from their role perspective and at a particular moment in the drama. For example, the space outside the outline may contain comments about Harry Potter as others see him and the interior space could contain his own feelings and views. This is a valuable convention for building a deeper understanding of a particular character and can be added to throughout a drama.

Teacher in role

This is the most powerful convention and involves the teacher engaging fully in the drama by taking various roles, e.g. leader, infiltrator, collaborator, messenger, vulnerable individual and so on. Through these, the teacher can support, extend and challenge the children's thinking from inside the drama. Every role has its own social status which gives access to different degrees of influence and power.

Thought tracking

In this convention, the private thoughts of individuals are shared publicly. This can be organised in various ways: the teacher can touch individuals on the shoulder during a freeze frame or halt an improvisation and ask them to voice their thoughts. Alternatively, the class could simultaneously speak aloud their thoughts and fears in a particular situation. Or the teacher and children in role, can give witness to the class and speak personally about recent events from a 'special' chair; members of the class can take turns in moving forward to stand behind the chair and express their thoughts from the character's perspective. This convention is useful to slow down the action and can prompt both deeper understanding of individual characters and very sensitive responses.

Writing in role

Different kinds of writing can emerge from the lived experience of the drama and can be written in role from the emotional stance and informed perspective of one of the characters - letters, diaries, messages, pamphlets, notes, even graffiti. Children often write with considerable urgency and passion in drama since they own the purpose and have a clearly imagined audience for their communication.

References and bibliography

Baldwin, P. and Fleming, K. (2003) *Teaching Literacy through Drama: Creative Approaches*. London: Routledge / Falmer.

Barrs, M. and Cork, V. (2001) *The Reader in the Writer: The Influence of Literature upon Writing at KS2*. London: CLPE.

Bennett, N., Wood, L. and Rogers, S. (1997) *Teaching Through Play: Teachers' thinking and classroom practice*. Oxford: Oxford University Press.

Booth, D. (1994) *Story drama: reading, writing and role playing across the curriculum*. Markham, Ontario: Pembroke.

Bruner, J. (1986) *Actual Minds, Possible Worlds*. Cambridge, Mass.: Harvard University Press.

Bunyan, P., Catron, J., Harrison, L., McEvoy, S., Moore, R., Welburn, B., and Williams, J. (2000) *Cracking Drama: Progression in Drama within English (5-16)*. York: York Publishing Services for NATE.

Claxton, G. (2000) A Sure Start for an Uncertain Education, *Early Education*, Spring 2000.

Cook, M. (2002) Bringing the outside in: using playful contexts to maximise young writers' capabilities in S. Ellis and C. Mills *Connecting Creating : New Ideas in teaching writing*. Shepreth, Herts: UKLA. pp 8-20

Costello, P. (2000) *Thinking Skills and Early Childhood Education*. London: David Fulton.

Craft, A. (2000) *Creativity across the Primary Curriculum*. London: Routledge.

Cremin, M. (2004) *The role of imagination in classroom drama*. Unpublished PhD dissertation, Canterbury Christ Church University College.

Cremin, T., Burnard, P., Craft, A. (2006), Pedagogy and possibility thinking in the early years, *International Journal of Thinking Skills and Creativity*, 1 (2): 108-119

DfEE (1998) *The National Literacy Strategy Framework for Teaching*. London: DfEE.

DfEE (1999) *All Our Futures: Creativity, Culture and Education*. London: DfEE.

DfEE/QCA (1999) *National Curriculum for English Programme of Study*. London: DfEE/QCA.

DfEE/QCA (2000) *The Curriculum Guidance for the Foundation Stage*. London: QCA/DfEE.

DfEE (1998) *The National Literacy Strategy Framework for Teaching*. London: DfEE.

DfES (2005) *Birth to Five*, London:DfES.

DfES (2006) *The National Literacy Strategy Framework for Teaching*. London: DfES.

Fisher, R. (1990) *Teaching Children to Think*. Oxford: Blackwell.

Friere, P. (1985) Reading the world and reading the word: an interview with Paulo Freire, *Language Arts* 62 (1): 15-21.

Galda, L. Pelligrini, D. and Cox, S. (1989) Preschoolers emerging literacy: A short term longitudinal study. *Research in the Teaching of English*, 23: 292-309.

Grainger, T. (1998) Drama and Reading: Illuminating their Interaction, *English in Education* 32 (1): 29-36.

Grainger, T. (2001a) Drama and Writing: Imagination on the Page, *The Primary English Magazine*. April, 2001: 6-10.

Grainger, T. (2001b) Drama and Writing: Imagination on the Page 2, *The Primary English Magazine*. June, 2001: 8-13.

Grainger, T. (2003a) Drama: Ambiguity and Uncertainty, in E. Bearne, H. Dombey and T. Grainger (Eds). *Classroom Interactions in Literacy*. Milton Keynes: Open University Press, pp105 - 114.

Grainger, T. (2003b) Let Drama build bridges between the subjects, *The Primary English Magazine*, pp 8-12.

Grainger, T. (2003c) Let Drama build Bridges to Non-Fiction Writing. *The Primary English Magazine*. pp 19-23.

Grainger, T. (2004) Drama and Writing: Enlivening their Prose, in P. Goodwin (Ed.) *Literacy through Creativity*. London: David Fulton.

Grainger, T. and Cremin, M. (2001) *Resourcing Classroom Drama 5-8*. Sheffield: NATE.

Grainger, T. and Kendal- Seatter, S. (2003) Drama and Spirituality: Some reflective connections, *The International Journal of Spirituality* Vol 8(1): 25-32.

Grainger, T., Goouch, K. and Lambirth, A. (2004) *Creativity and Writing*. London: Routledge.

Griffiths, J. (1991) *An Early Start to Drama*. London: Simon and Schuster.

Hall, N. and Robinson, A. (1995) *Exploring Play and Writing in the Early Years*. London: David Fulton.

Hall, N. and Abbott, L. (1993) *Play and the National Curriculum*. London: Hodder and Stoughton.

Heathcote, D. and Bolton G. (1995) *Drama for Learning: Dorothy Heathcote's Mantle of the Expert Approach to Education*. London: Heinemann.

Hendy, L. and Toon, L. (2001) *Supporting Drama and Imaginative Play in the Early Years*. Buckingham: Open University Press.

McNaughton, M.J. (1997) Drama and Children's Writing : a study of the influence of drama on the imaginative writing of primary school children, *Research in Drama Education* 12 (1):55-86.

Neelands, J. (1992) *Learning Through Imagined Experience (Teaching English in the National Curriculum)*. London: Hodder Arnold.

Neelands, J. (1998) *Beginning Drama 11-14*. London: David Fulton.

Neelands, J. (2000) *Structuring Drama Work*. Cambridge: Cambridge University Press.

O'Neill, C. (1995) *Drama Worlds: a Framework for Process Drama*. London: Heinemann.

Parker-Rees, R. (1999) Protecting Playfulness, in Abbott, L. and Moylett, H. (eds.) *Early Education Transformed*. London: Falmer Press, pp 61 - 72.

QCA (1998) *Education for Citizenship and the Teaching of Democracy in Schools*. London; QCA.

QCA (1999) *Teaching Speaking and Listening at Key Stages 1 and 2*. Sudbury: QCA Publications.

Rosenblatt, L. (1978) *The Reader, the Text and the Poem: the Transactional Theory of Literacy at Work*. Carbondale, Illinois: South Illinois Press.

Singer, D. and Singer, J (1990) *The House of Make Believe*. Harvard: Harvard University Press.

Taylor, P. (1995) *Pre-text and Storydrama: the Artistry of Cecily O'Neill and David Booth*. Australia: NADIE.

Taylor, P. and Warner, C.D. (2006) *Structure and Spontaneity: the process drama of Cecily O'Neil*. Stoke on Trent: Trentham.

Toye, N. and Prendiville, F. (2000) *Drama and Traditional Story for the Early Years*. London: Routledge Falmer.

Winston, J.(1998) *Drama, Narrative and Moral Education*. London: Falmer Press

Winston, J. (2000) *Drama, Literacy and Moral Education 5-11*. London: David Fulton.

Winston, J. and Tandy, M. (1998) *Beginning Drama 4-11*. London: David Fulton.

Wood, E.A. and Attfield, J. (1996) *Play, Learning and the Early Childhood Curriculum*. London: Paul Chapman Publishing.

UKLA Minibook Series

Minibooks now no longer in print

Genres in the Classroom Alison B. Littlefair

Running Family Reading Groups Sue Beverton, Ann Stuart,
Morag Hunter-Carsch
and Cecelia Oberist

Teaching Handwriting Peter Smith

Teaching Spelling Brigid Smith

Supporting Struggling Readers Diana Bentley and Dee Reid

Phonological Awareness Frances James

Exploring the Writing of Genres Beverley Derewianka

**The Power of Words: Guidelines for
improving spelling and vocabulary** Norma Mudd

Reading to Find Out Helen Arnold

**Moving Towards Literacy with
Environmental Print** Linda Miller

**English as an Additional Language:
Language and literacy development** Constant Leung

UKLA MINIBOOKS

Minibook 27

Practical Bilingual Strategies for Multilingual Classrooms

By Tözün Issa and Alayne Öztürk

One of the challenges faced by Early Years and Primary teachers today is catering effectively for the variety of needs within their classrooms and settings. It can indeed be very challenging to provide appropriate and stimulating activities to facilitate access to the curriculum for bilingual children. The primary aim of this book is to provide some guidance for practitioners through tried and tested strategies to support bilingual learners in the appropriate Key Stages. Suggested activities reflect children's various linguistic and cultural experiences and highlight the importance of maintaining the role of the home language. The practical examples shown in this book reflect positive practice observed both at home and in some schools where such experiences are used most effectively.

About the Authors

Tözün Issa was a classroom teacher for twelve years, and an EMAG Consultant for six years in the boroughs of Tower Hamlets and Lambeth. He completed a PhD on the subject of bilingual education and is currently a lecturer at London Metropolitan University, with a specialism in bilingual education. He is the Director of the Centre for Multilingualism in Education, based at the University.

Alayne Öztürk was a primary classroom teacher for nine years, and she taught English as an Additional Language in Turkey for two years. She is currently Primary Programme Director for Initial Teacher Education at London Metropolitan University. She specialises in literacy education, and is an executive member of the Centre for Multilingualism in Education, based at the university.

Minibooks are available from
UKLA Publications, 4th Floor, Attenborough Building, University of Leicester, Leicester LE1 7RH.

47